The Young Guitarist

Sequential Music for Group & Private Lessons
Volume 1

Revised Edition

Editing and Arranging: **Johnny Peña**
Original Works: **Johnny Peña**
Cover Artwork: **Jenny Peña**

Table of Contents

Johnny Peña is a guitarist and music educator with fifteen years of experience working with students of all ages, from beginners at the elementary music level to future music educators at the college level. After earning his MM from the University of Texas at San Antonio in 2014 under the direction of Dr. Matthew Dunne, he has continued to teach in the San Antonio and Austin areas. In his years as an educator, he has taught private guitar lessons, guitar ensembles, guitar literature, music theory, guitar pedagogy, and elementary music. Most recently, he has had the pleasure to be a part of the faculty at two distinguished universities: UTSA (2018-2022) and the Baptist University of the Americas (2016-2018). Additionally, he also served as the guitar director for the UTSA String Project and led weekly String Project guitar pedagogy classes (2018-2022).

Mr. Peña has participated in many international guitar competitions and earned first prize in the Mountain View College Festival and Competition (2018) and third prize in the Lone Star Guitar Festival and Competition (2017). He has also had the pleasure to participate in master classes with many world-class guitarists, including David Russell, Berta Rojas, Xuefei Yang, Adam Holzman, Fabio Montomoli, Bill Kannengiser, and more. One of his favorite performances was when he was invited to perform the "Concierto de Aranjuez" at the Majestic Theatre in San Antonio, Texas, with Symphony Viva in November 2021.

When he isn't teaching, Mr. Peña enjoys spending time with his wife, Jenny, and their son, Desmond. Outside of music, he is a foodie and enjoys skateboarding and gaming. Mr. Peña is also an active real estate agent in San Antonio and Austin.

Photo Credit: William "Bill" McCrary

A NOTE FROM THE AUTHOR

This is Volume 1 of a collection of sequential guitar music for group or private lessons. Most pieces in this series are arrangements of folk songs, and the rest are original works I composed. I have spent about ten years compiling these materials through my work with students in both group and private lesson settings.

I first began this collection of arrangements and compositions during my time working as a graduate student with the String Project at the University of Texas at San Antonio (UTSA) in 2012. The UTSA String Project provides low-cost orchestra and guitar lessons to children in the communities of San Antonio. UTSA college students are hired by the String Project to teach primarily group classes, and in the process the UTSA faculty members provide helpful resources and feedback to guide and aid the student teachers' development.

Once I graduated from UTSA, I was offered the incredible opportunity to join the staff at my alma mater as a professor (2017-2022). Part of my role was to serve as the guitar director for the String Project program I had once taught in as a student teacher. As guitar director, my love for arranging continued to grow, as did my desire to create a group guitar curriculum. Over the years, many students have learned from my collection, and many of the String Project teachers have since taught other students using my materials. I greatly enjoyed the opportunity to be in an environment where I was inspired to create arrangements and write original music that matched both the students' and teachers' evolving needs.

I would like to give a special thank-you to my wife, Jenny Peña, who is an amazing music educator and performer herself. I am endlessly grateful that she shares her musical successes and new teaching ideas with me. She continues to inspire me to experiment with new approaches to teaching music.

I cannot thank my family enough, including my mom, Socorro Peña, for always supporting my interest in music. I would not be where I am today without their support.

I would also like to give a special thank-you to my mentors, professors, and friends I have met along my journey: Dr. Matthew Dunne, Dr. Eugene Dowdy, Dr. Kristen Pellegrino, and Dr. Susan Dill. They have each helped me improve my musicianship skills as both a performer and an educator. I would also like to thank my "guitar crew" I met during my master's program at UTSA as well as any musician I have crossed paths with over the last ten years. You all have impacted and inspired my musical journey by sharing your craft and expertise.

Lastly, I would like to thank all the teachers and students I've had the privilege of working with over the years. They have contributed greatly to my musical journey, and I cannot express how grateful I am for their help.

<u>A NOTE TO THE TEACHER</u>

Thank you for choosing my book for your guitar lessons! In creating this series, I have drawn inspiration from two pedagogues that have greatly influenced my teaching: Shinichi Suzuki and Aaron Shearer.

Three aspects that I include in my method from Suzuki's approach to teaching are:

- Learning a shared repertoire.
- Utilizing sound before sight, especially during the early stages of music learning.
- Creating a growth mindset by using positive reinforcement.

Two aspects that I include from Shearer's approach are:

- Using a sequence of right-hand technique inspired by Aaron Shearer's approach to guitar pedagogy.
- Using fixed Do as a form of visualization of the music and the guitar fretboard.

The sequential collection of music in Volume 1 is arranged for two to three parts. Each part has room for growth through various aspects of musicianship skills and technique, and this book is split up into three units.

<u>UNIT 1</u>

<u>Right-Hand Technique</u>
In my years of teaching, I have observed that the right-hand thumb is an easy finger for most students to control in a manner that is relaxed and musical. As such, I have arranged all the guitar parts in Unit 1 for the right-hand thumb.

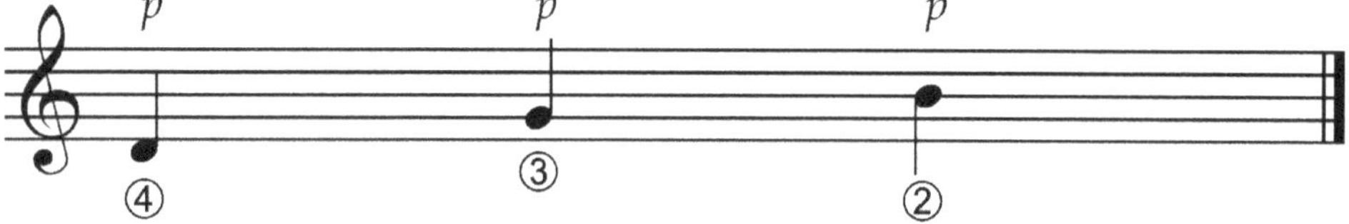

<u>Left-Hand Technique</u>
Unit 1 focuses on natural notes in first position on the 2nd, 3rd, and 4th strings.

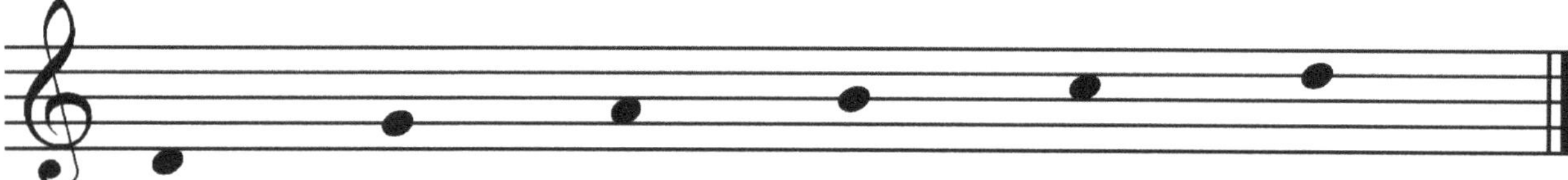

<u>Music Literacy</u>
I am a believer of allowing students to experience musical concepts before adding labels, also known as "sound before sight." Rote teaching is the most effective way to introduce music literacy concepts during the first phase of lessons. By the end of Unit 1, students will be able to read natural notes in first position on the staff on the 2nd, 3rd, and 4th strings.

<u>Ensemble Skills</u>
In Unit 1, there are three distinct parts written for each piece: melody, harmony, and bass. After students have learned and internalized each part, they may begin playing in an ensemble setting.

Suggested division of parts for ensemble practice in a group setting:

Example 1:
Group 1 – Plays melody first, harmony second, bass third.
Group 2 – Plays harmony first, bass second, melody third.
Group 3 – Plays bass first, melody second, harmony third.
Teacher – Plays accompaniment.

Example 2:
Group 1 – Plays melody first, harmony second, bass third.
Group 2 – Plays bass first, melody second, harmony third.
Teacher – Plays accompaniment

> *In a studio or private lesson setting, the teacher can have the student play the parts individually first. Then the teacher and student can play together and alternate parts.

UNIT 2

<u>Right Hand Technique</u>
Unit 2 introduces alternating rest strokes with IM. Right-hand thumb strokes are incorporated into the bass lines.

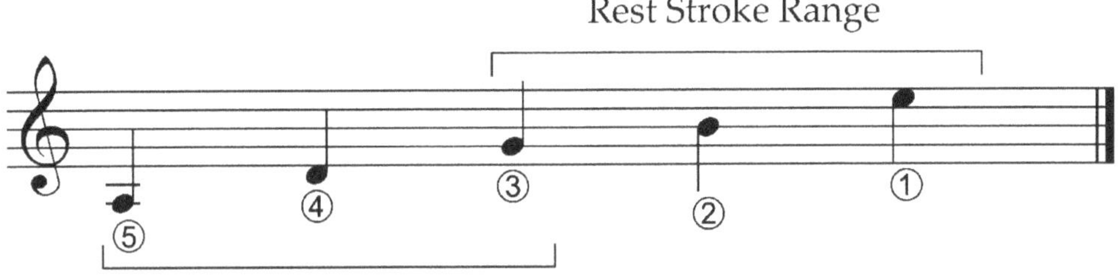

<u>LH Technique</u>
Unit 2 introduces the first string notes E (Mi), F (Fa), and G (So). The fifth string note C (Do) and fourth string E (Mi) and F (Fa) are also introduced.

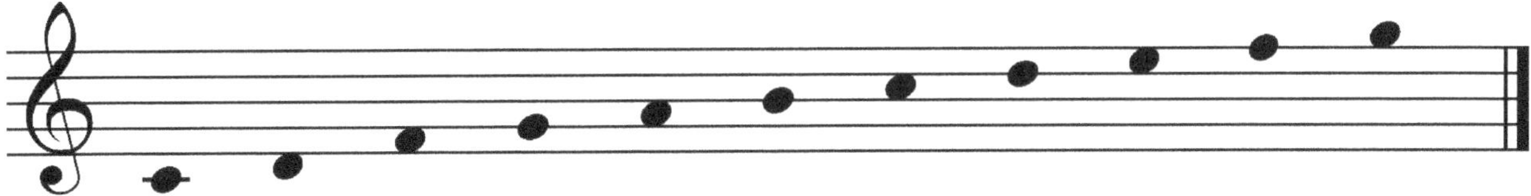

<u>Music Literacy</u>
By the end of Unit 2, students will be able to read natural notes in first position on the staff on the 1st, 2nd, 3rd, 4th, and 5th strings.

<u>Ensemble Skills</u>
Each piece is written for three parts. Students will continue to develop ensemble skills through new repertoire.

UNIT 3

<u>Right-Hand Technique</u>
In Unit 3, dyads (two-note chords) played with right-hand index and middle fingers (IM) are introduced with a separate part included in each arrangement. Right-hand thumb strokes are incorporated into the melody and bass lines.

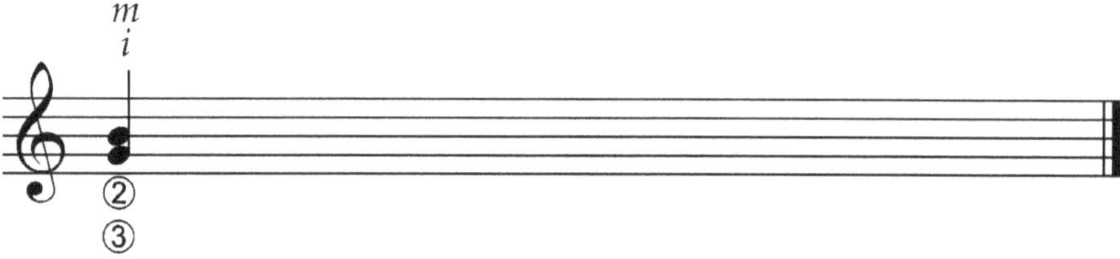

<u>Left-Hand Technique</u>
All notes in this unit are in first position.

<u>Music Literacy</u>
By the end of Unit 3, students will be able to read natural notes in first position on the staff on the 1st, 2nd, 3rd, 4th, and 5th strings. The symbols for sharps and flats are introduced in this unit.

<u>Ensemble Skills</u>
Each piece is written for three parts. Students will continue to develop ensemble skills through new repertoire.

UNIT 1

Anatomy of a Guitar

Right and Left Hand Finger Names

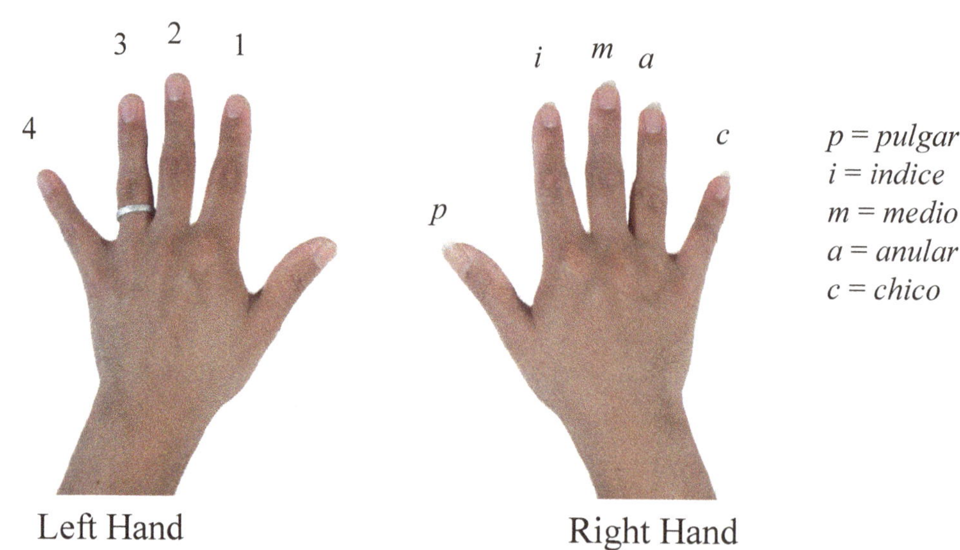

Holding the Guitar: Playing Position

Free Strokes with the Thumb (*p*) on G (So) and D (Re)

*The right-hand fingers should be relaxed before and after the strings are plucked.

G (So) - 3rd String
- The right-hand thumb (*p*) is planted on the 3rd string.
- The tips of the index (*i*), middle (*m*), and ring (*a*) fingers gently rest on the 1st string.
- The *i*, *m*, and *a* fingers remain curved and relaxed.

- The right-hand thumb (*p*) plays and follows through to the index finger (*i*).

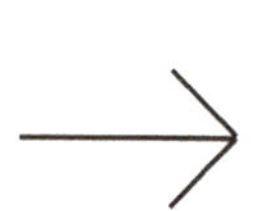

D (Re) - 4th String
- The right-hand thumb (*p*) is planted on the 4th string.

- The right-hand thumb (*p*) plays and follows through to the index (*i*).

Practice Playing G (So) and D (Re)

Follow these steps for each phrase below:
1. Sing the solfege syllabes (or alphabet note names) and visualize the notes.
2. Sing and play the example with the right-hand.

Hot Cross Buns

English Folk Song
arr. Johnny Peña

Bass Line

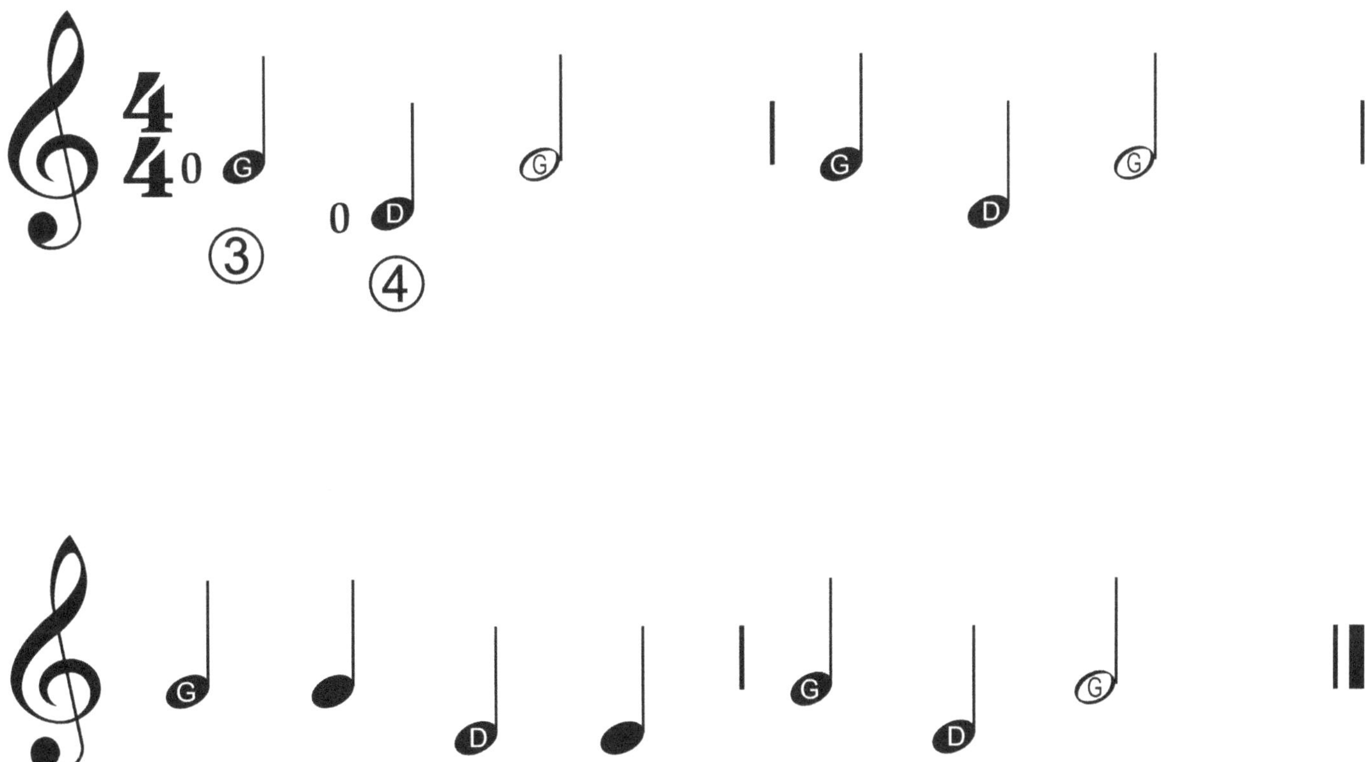

<u>B (Ti) and A (La)</u>

B (Ti)
2nd String

- The right-hand thumb (*p*) is planted on the 2nd string.

A (La)
3rd String
2nd Fret

- The left-hand 2nd finger presses down on the fret.

Left Hand Posture

1. The pad of the left-hand thumb is lightly placed behind the neck. The thumb should be vertical, not sideways.
2. The left-hand wrist is centered, not angled.
3. The left-hand fingers (1, 2, 3, and 4) maintain a C shape at all times.
4. The left-hand fingers (1, 2, 3, and 4) are curved and relaxed.
5. All notes are fretted with the tips of the fingers, not the pads.

Practice Playing B (Ti) and A (La)

Follow these steps for each phrase below:
1. Sing the solfege syllabes (or alphabet note names) and visualize the notes.
2. Sing and play with the right-hand only.
3. Sing and fret along with the left-hand only.
4. Play through the example with both hands.

Hot Cross Buns

English Folk Song
arr. Johnny Peña

Melody Line

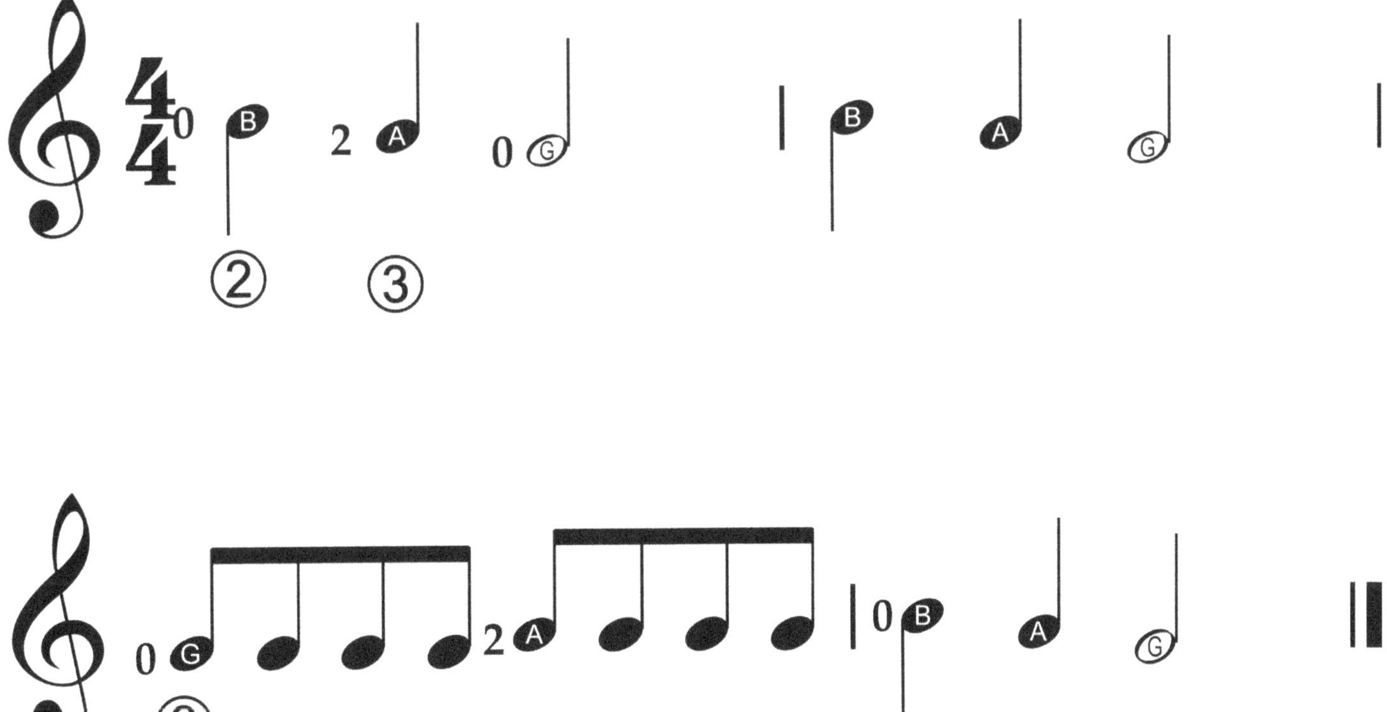

D (Re) and C (Do)

D (Re)
2nd String
3rd Fret

- The left-hand 3rd finger presses down on the fret.

D (Do)
2nd String
1st Fret

- The left-hand 1st finger presses down on the fret.

D (Re) and C (Do)

Follow these steps for each phrase below:
1. Sing the solfege syllabes (or alphabet note names) and visualize the notes.
2. Sing and play with the right-hand only.
3. Sing and fret along with the left-hand only.
4. Play through the example with both hands.

Hot Cross Buns

English Folk Song
arr. Johnny Peña

Harmony Line

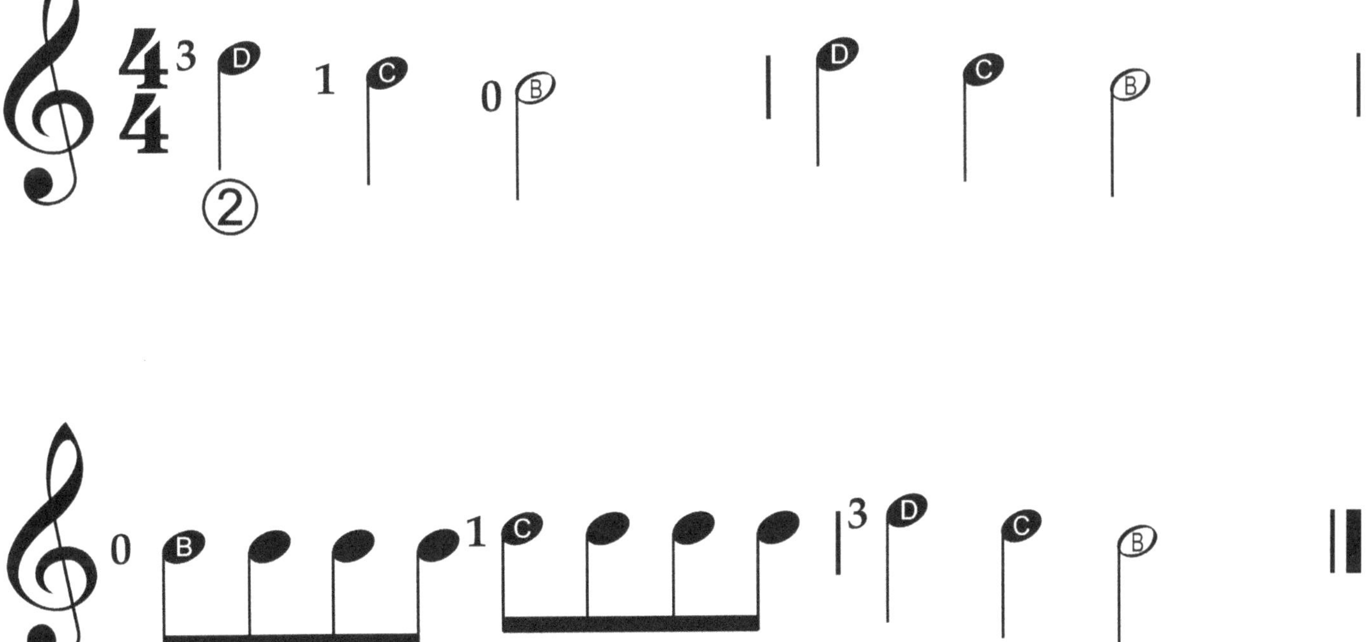

Notes used in this piece

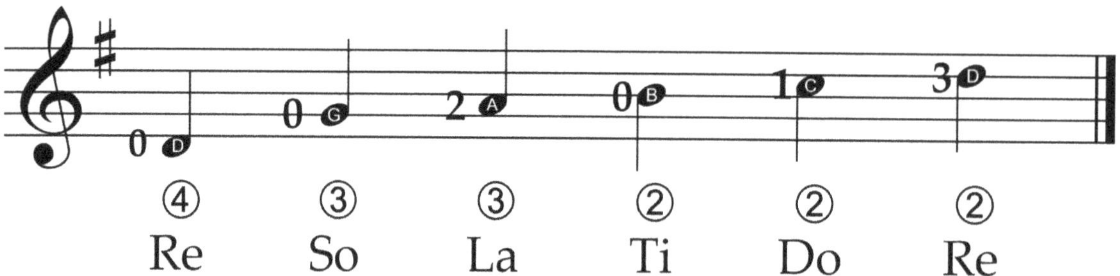

Hot Cross Buns

English Folk Song
arr. Johnny Peña

Melody

Harmony

Bass

Teacher Accompaniment

Follow these steps for each part in Hot Cross Buns:
1. Sing the solfege syllabes (or alphabet note names) and visualize the notes.
2. Sing and play with the right hand only.
3. Sing and fret along with the left hand only.
4. Play through the piece with both hands.

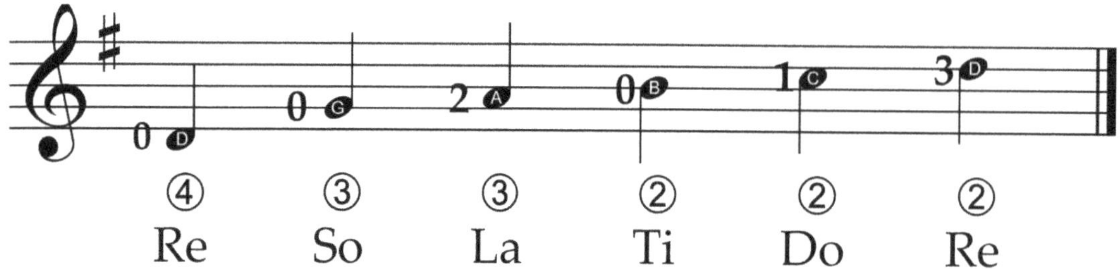

Mary Had a Little Lamb

English Folk Song
arr. Johnny Peña

Melody

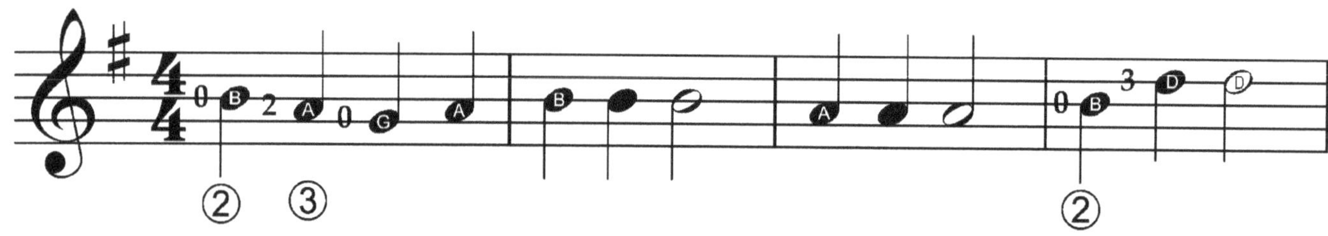

5

Bass

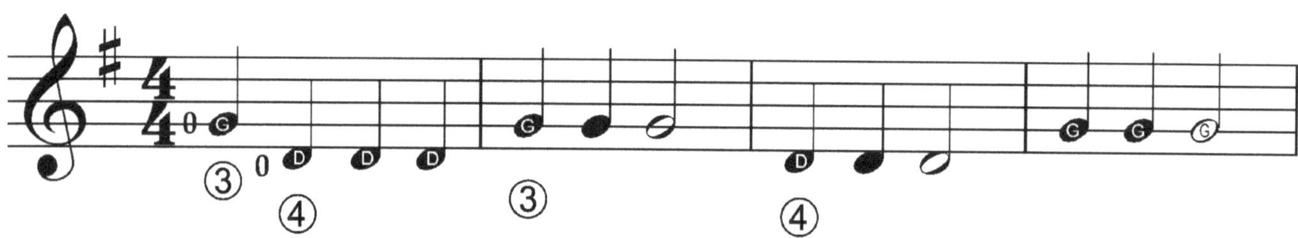

5

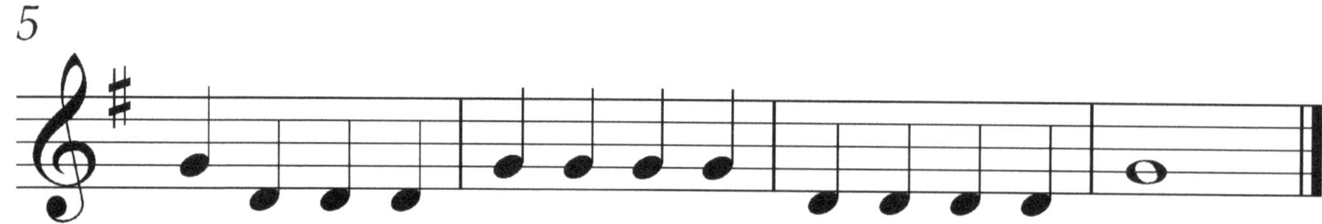

Harmony

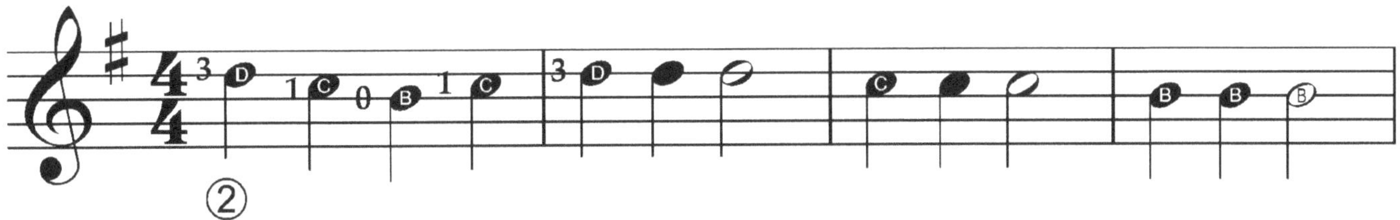

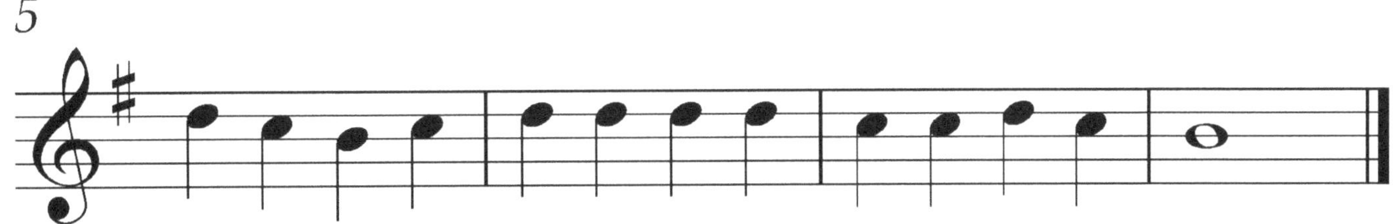

Teacher Accompaniment

Remember to follow these steps for each part in Mary Had a Little Lamb:
1. Sing the solfege syllabes (or alphabet note names) and visualize the notes.
2. Sing and play with the right-hand only.
3. Sing and fret along with the left-hand only.
4. Play through the piece with both hands.

Notes used in this piece

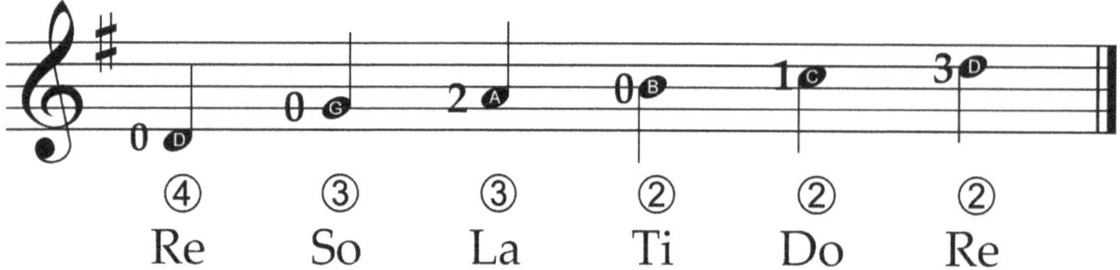

Lightly Row

German/English Folk Song
arr. Johnny Peña

Melody

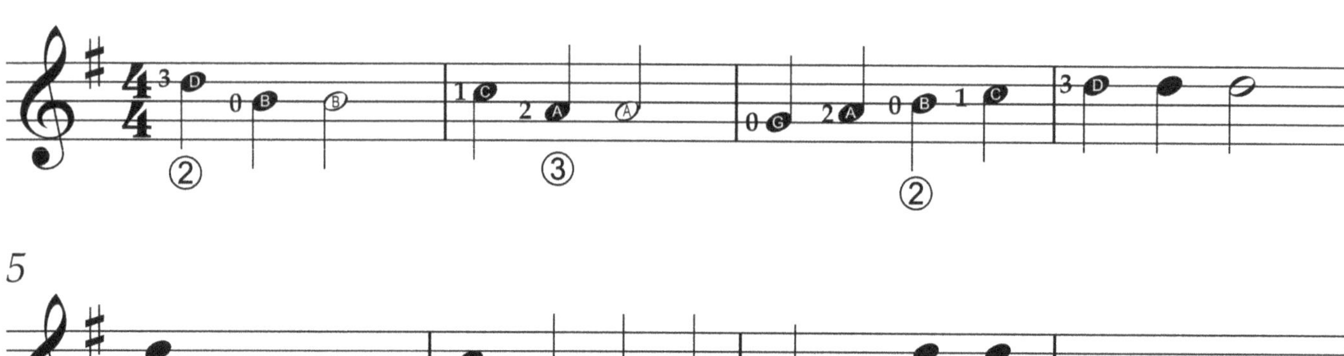

5

9

13

Follow these steps for each part in Lightly Row:
1. Sing the solfege syllabes (or alphabet note names) and visualize the notes.
2. Sing and play with the right-hand only.
3. Sing and fret along with the left-hand only.
4. Play through the piece with both hands.

Lightly Row

Harmony

Lightly Row

Lightly Row
German/English Folk Song
arr. Johnny Peña
Teacher Accompaniment

UNIT 2

Alternating Rest Strokes with IM

1. *p* is planted on the 6th string (or 5th string). *i* is planted on the 1st string while it is extended and slightly curved.

2. *i* plays the 1st string by pressing down until it is plucked, then it rests on the 2nd string.

m gently hovers over the 1st string.

3. *m* plants on the 1st string.

4. *m* presses down into the 1st string until it is plucked, then it rests on the 2nd string.

i gently hovers over the 1st string.

5. *i* plays the 1st string by pressing down into the string until it is plucked, then it rests on the 2nd string.

m gently hovers over the 1st string.

Notated Example

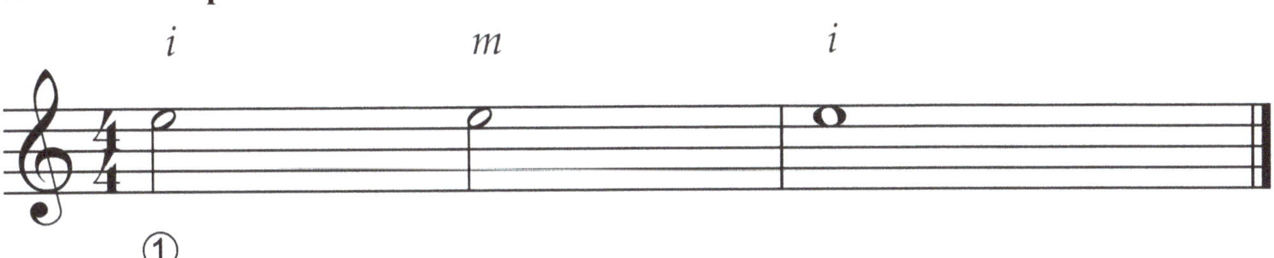

1st String E (Mi), F (Fa), and G (So)

These new notes will be incorporated into the melody line of the upcoming piece titled "Pepperoni Pizza," which can be found on page 21.

E (Mi)
Open 1st String

- The right-hand index finger is planted on the 1st string.

F (Fa)
1st String
1st Fret

- The left-hand 1st finger presses down on the fret.

G (So)
1st String
3rd Fret

- The left-hand 3rd finger presses down on the fret.

Pepperoni Pizza

♩=40-50

Johnny Peña

Melody

Harmony

Teacher Accompaniment

This page is intentionally left blank.

Introducing and Playing 4th String E (Mi)

The 4th string E (Mi) will be used in the upcoming bass line of the song "Star Light, Star Bright," which can be found on page 25.

E (Mi)
4th String
2nd Fret

- The left-hand 2nd finger presses down on the fret.

Ex. 1

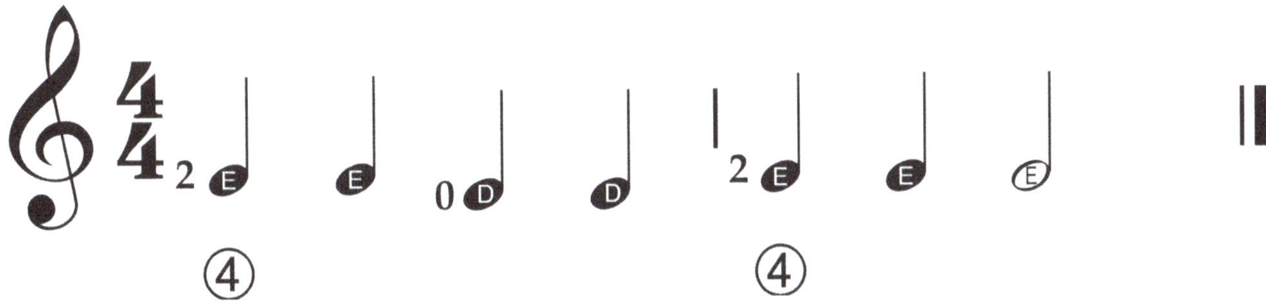

Ex. 2

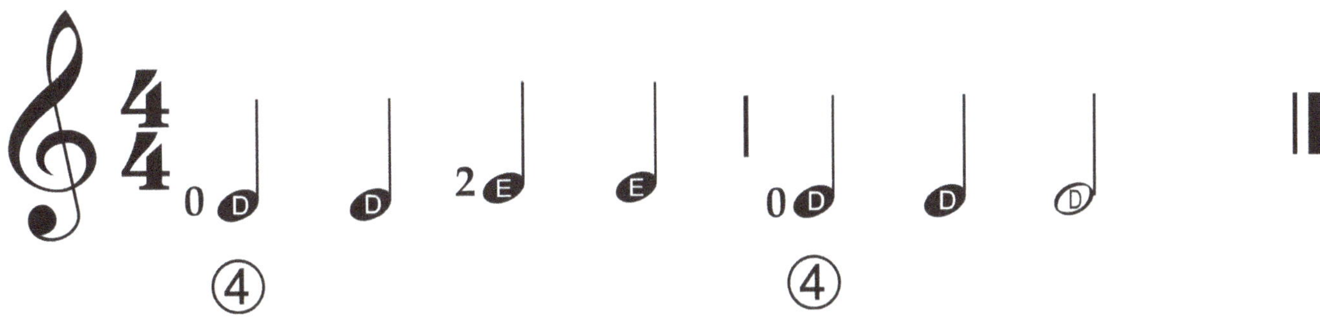

Notes used in this piece

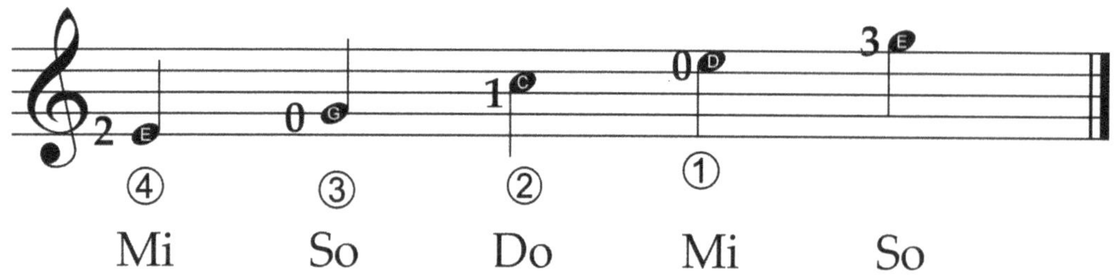

Star Light, Star Bright

American Folk Song
arr. Johnny Peña

Melody

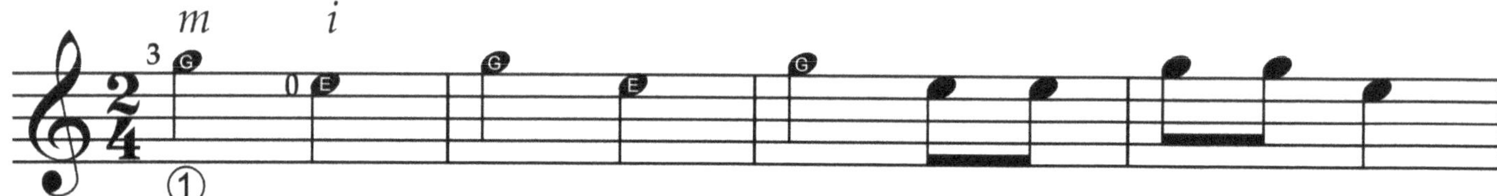

5

Harmony

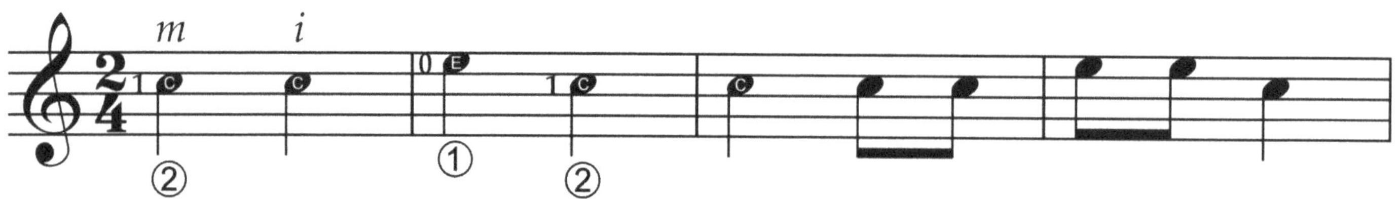

5

Bass

Teacher Accompaniment

Remember to follow these steps for each part in Star Light, Star Bright:
1. Sing the solfege syllabes (or alphabet note names) and visualize the notes.
2. Sing and play with the right-hand only.
3. Sing and fret along with the left-hand only.
4. Play through the piece with both hands.

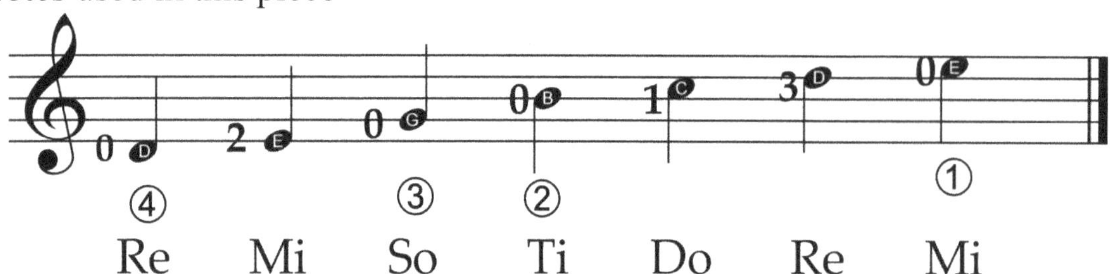

Los Pollitos

Mexican Folk Song
arr. Johnny Peña

Melody

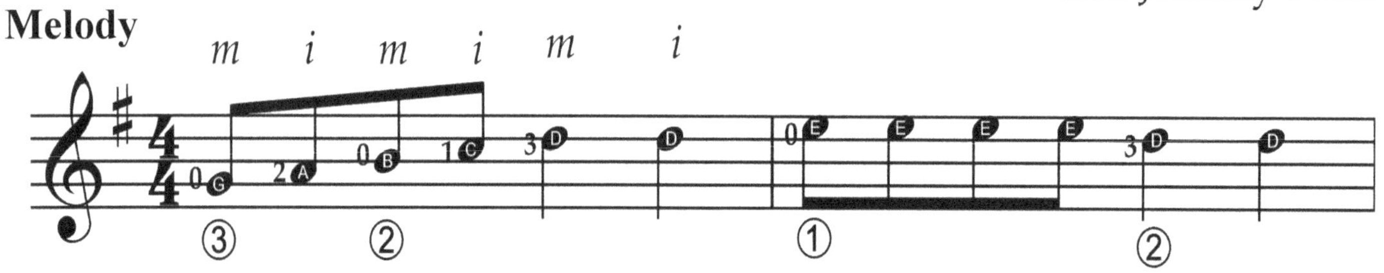

3

Harmony

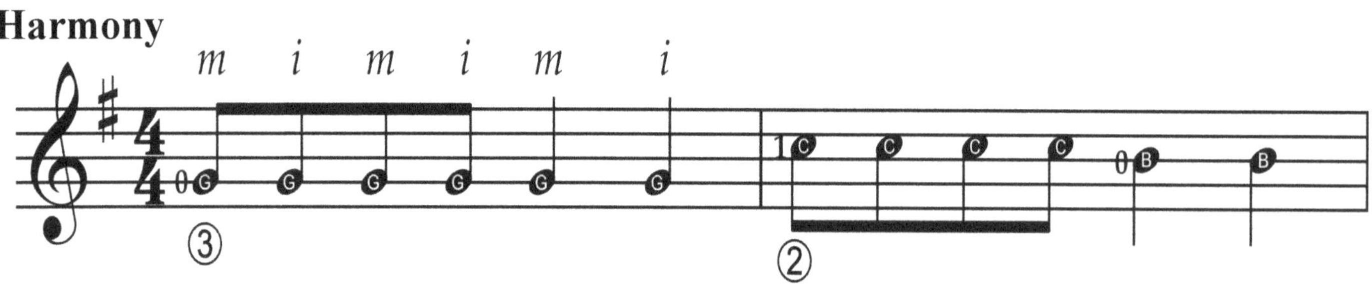

3

Bass

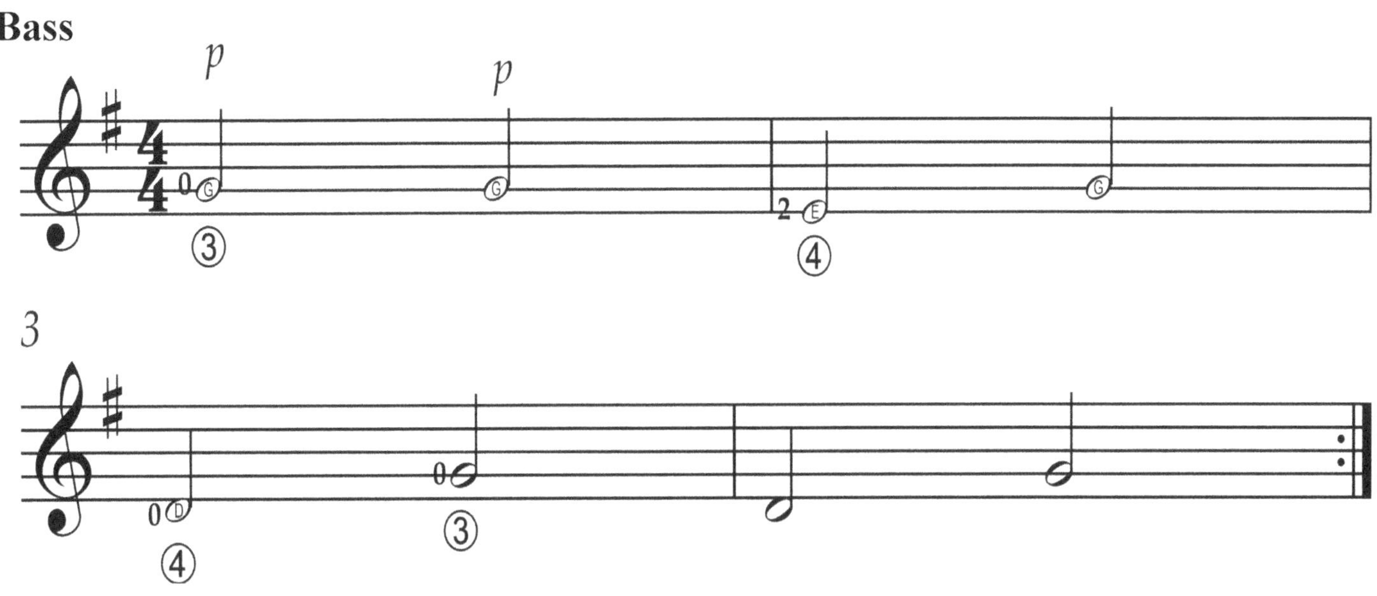

Teacher Accompaniment

Remember to follow these steps for each part in Los Pollitos:
1. Sing the solfege syllabes (or alphabet note names) and visualize the notes.
2. Sing and play with the right-hand only.
3. Sing and fret along with the left-hand only.
4. Play through the piece with both hands.

5th String C (Do)

The 5th string C (Do) will be used in the bass line of the upcoming piece titled "Sur le Pont D'Avignon," which can be found on page 31.

C (Do)
5th String
3rd Fret

- The left-hand 3rd finger presses down on the fret.

Ex. 1

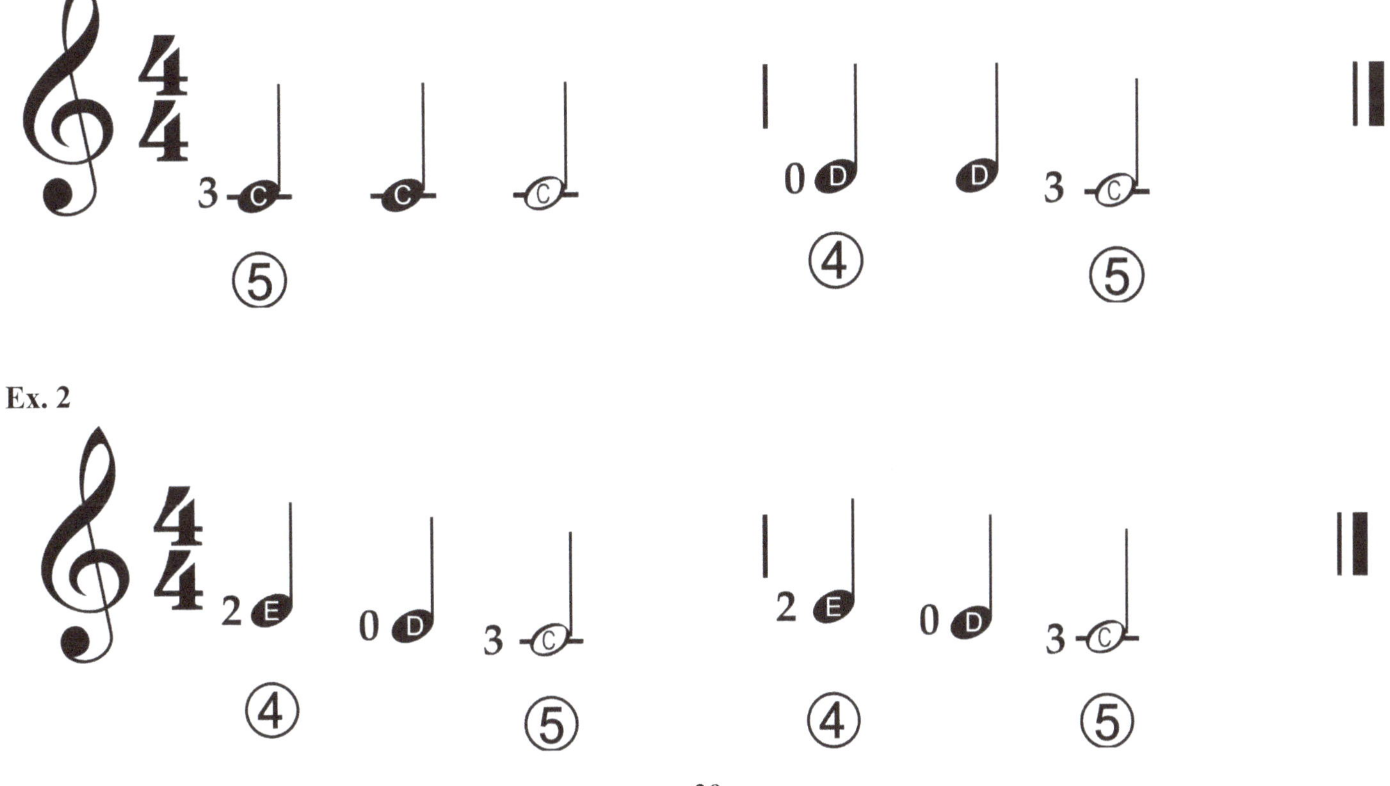

Ex. 2

Notes used in this piece

Sur le Pont D'Avingnon

French Folk Song
arr. Johnny Peña

Melody

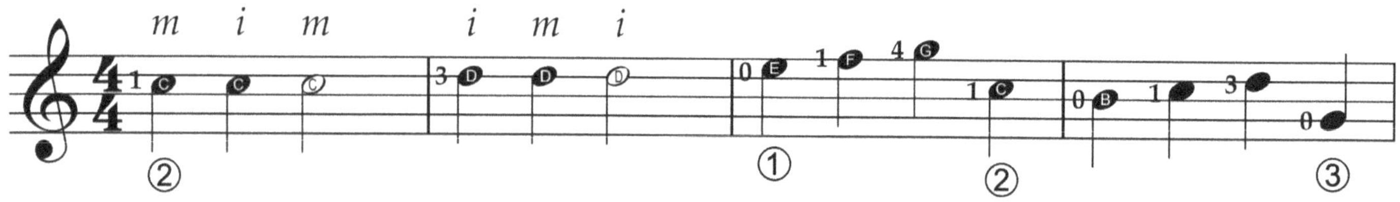

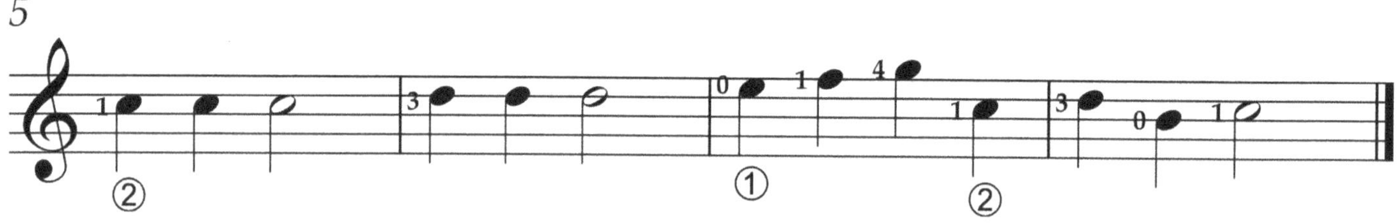

Harmony

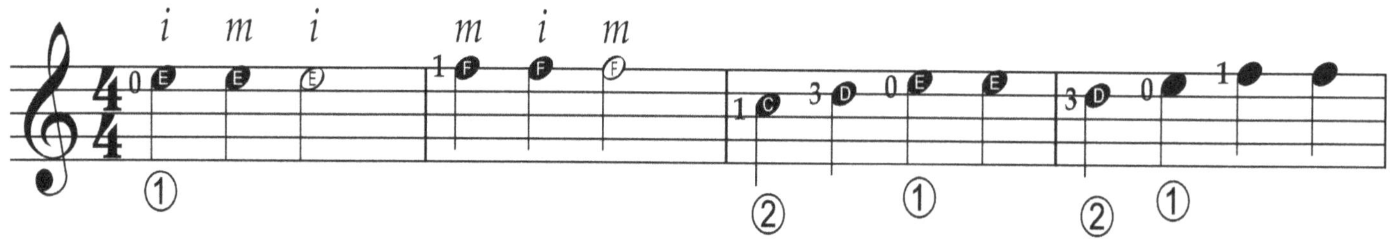

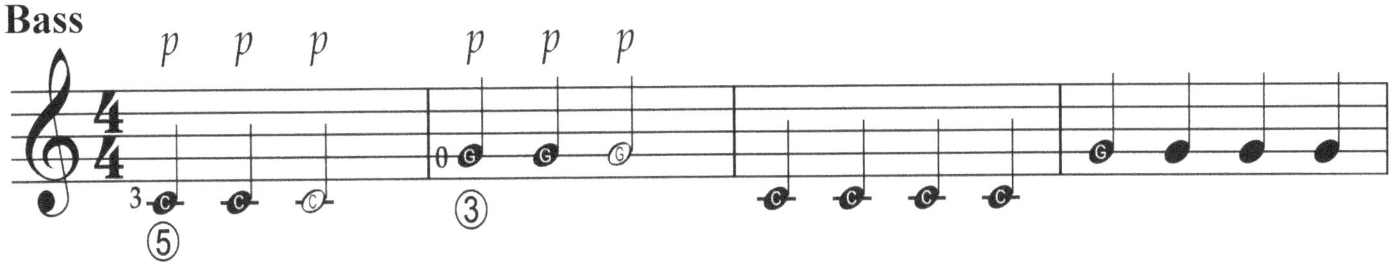

Teacher Accompaniment

Remember to follow these steps for each part in Sur le Pont D'Avingnon:
1. Sing the solfege syllabes (or alphabet note names) and visualize the notes.
2. Sing and play with the right-hand only.
3. Sing and fret along with the left-hand only.
4. Play through the piece with both hands.

El Sube y Baja

Mexican Folk Song
arr. Johnny Peña

Melody

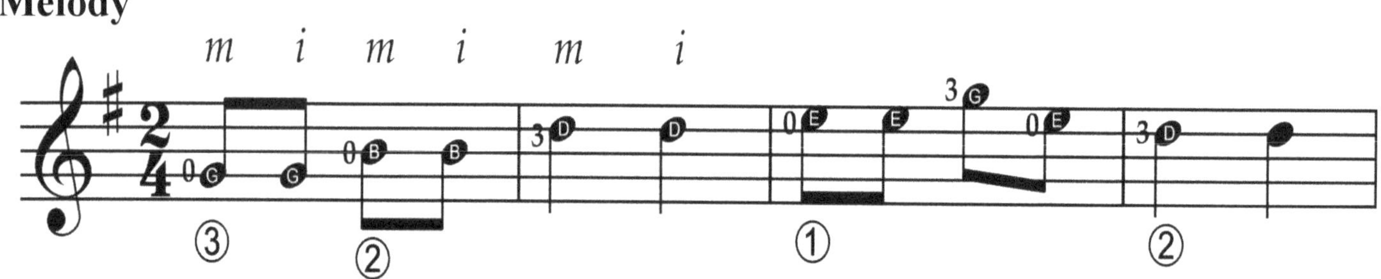

Harmony

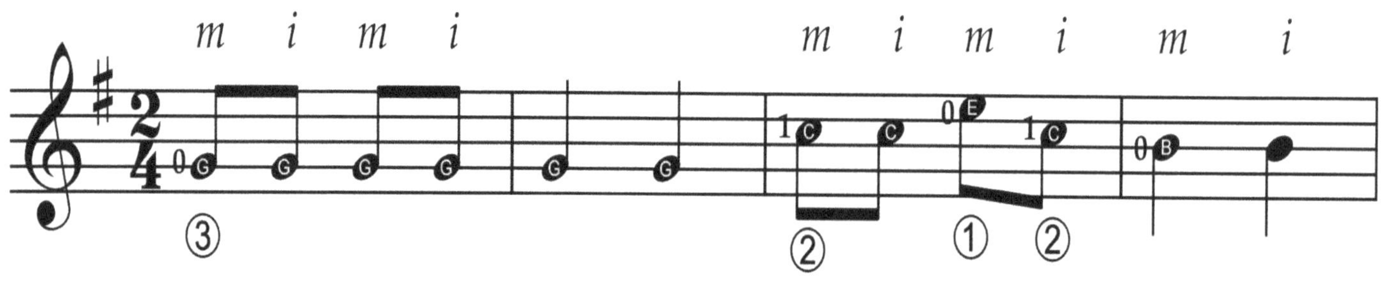

Bass

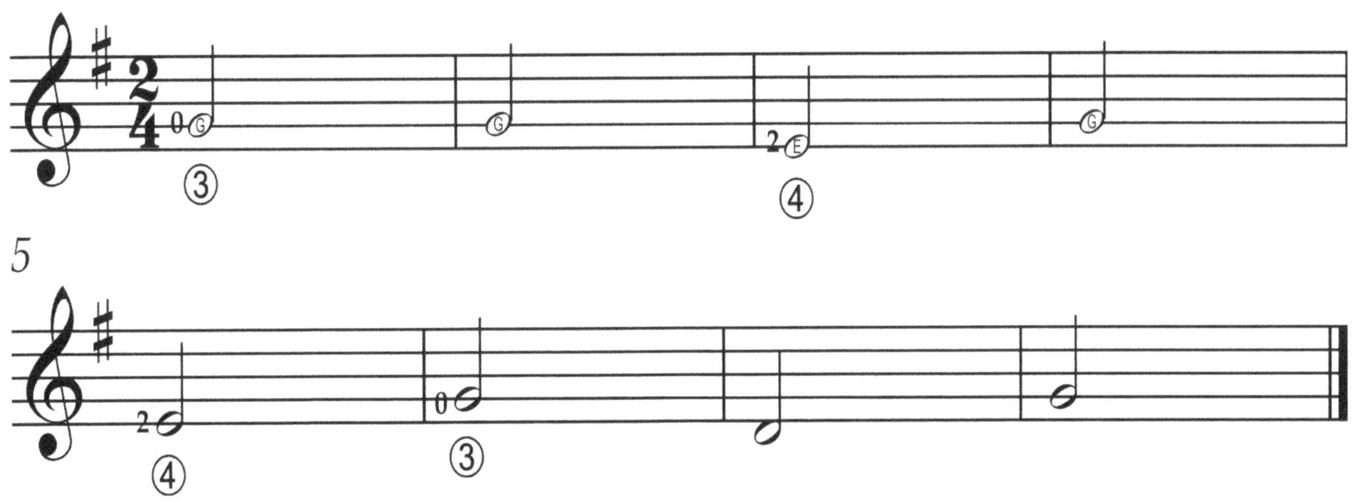

Teacher Accompaniment

Remember to follow these steps for each part in El Sube y Baja:
1. Sing the solfege syllabes (or alphabet note names) and visualize the notes.
2. Sing and play with the right-hand only.
3. Sing and fret along with the left-hand only.
4. Play through the piece with both hands.

Introducing and Playing 4th String F (Fa)

F (Fa)
4th String
3rd Fret

- The left-hand 3rd finger
  presses down on the fret.

C Major Scale

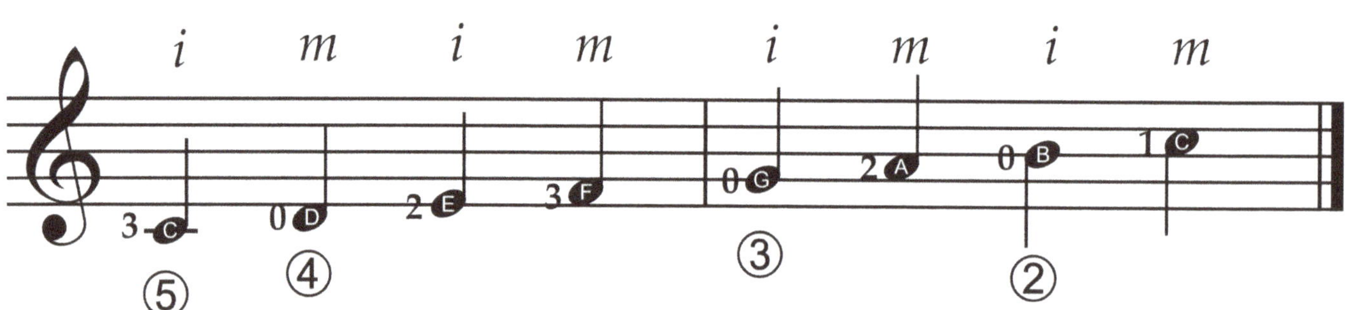

Rhythm Time: Food Chants

Practice the examples below with your teacher. These rhythms will be used in the upcoming piece "Los Xtoles."

Ex. 1

Ex. 2

Ex. 3

Notes used in this piece

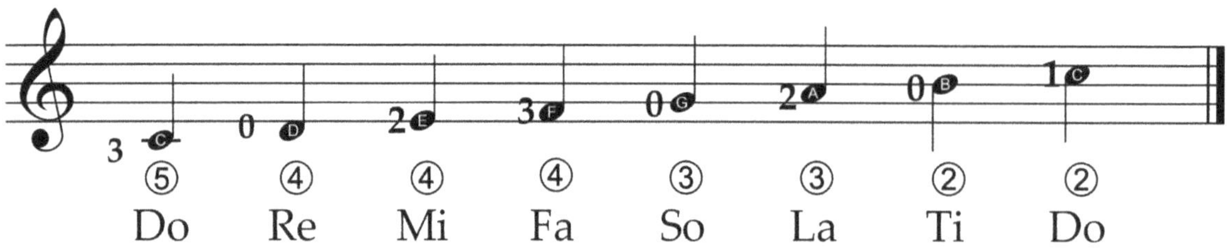

Los Xtoles

Mexican Folk Song
arr. Johnny Peña

Melody

Los Xtoles

Harmony Part

Mexican Folk Song
arr. Johnny Peña

Follow these steps for each part in Los Xtoles:
1. Sing the solfege syllabes (or alphabet note names) and visualize the notes.
2. Sing and play with the right-hand only.
3. Sing and fret along with the left-hand only.
4. Play through the piece with both hands.

Los Xtoles

Bass Part

Mexican Folk Song
arr. Johnny Peña

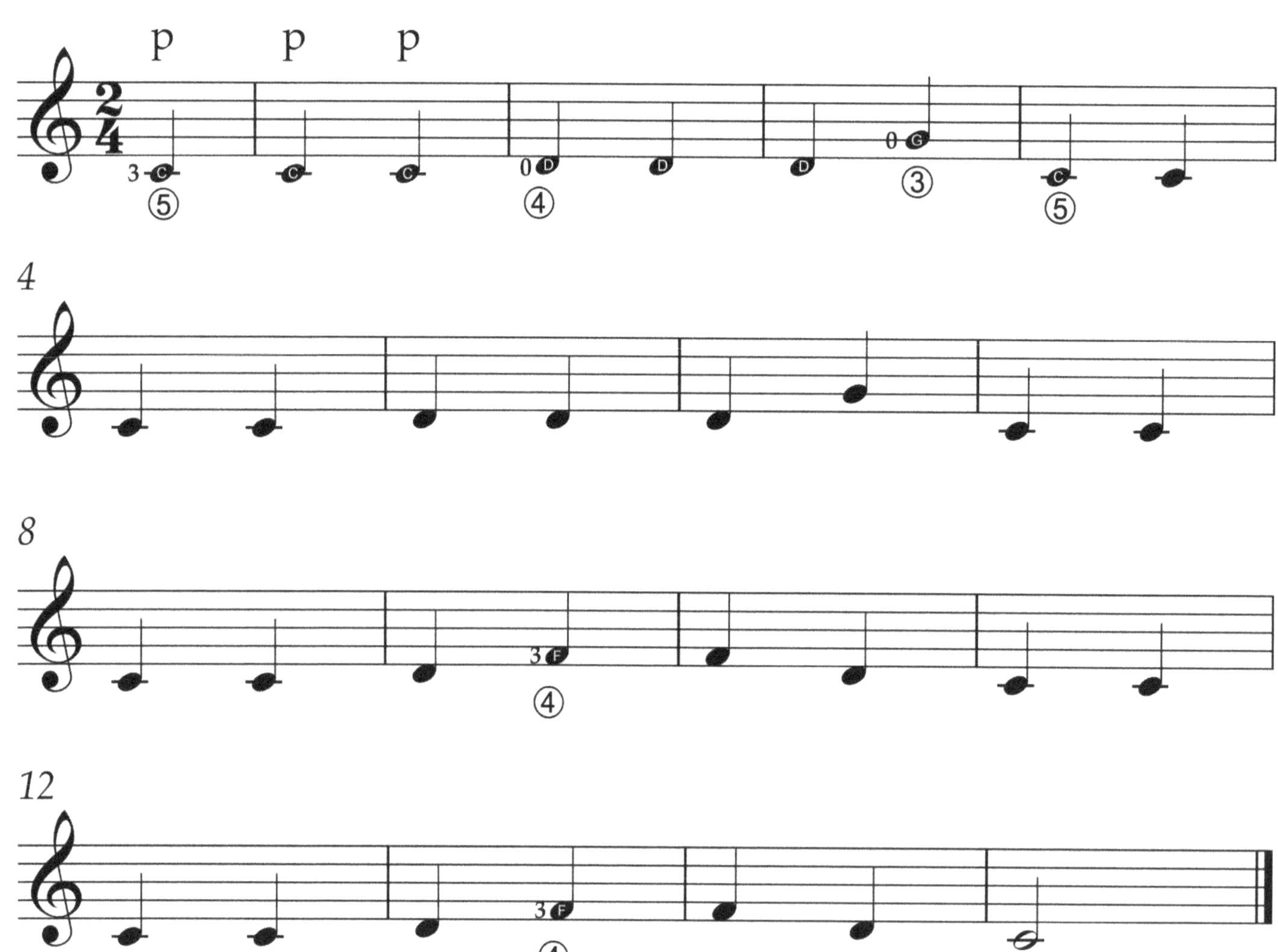

Teacher Accompaniment

UNIT 3

Free Strokes with the Index and Middle (*im*)

Playing the 3rd string G (So) and 2nd string B (Ti)

1. *i* and *m* are planted on the 3rd and 2nd strings, respectively.

p is planted on the 5th string or the 4th string.

2. *i* and *m* play and follow through into the palm with the pads of the fingers along with *a* and *c*.

IM Free Stroke Parts Added to Repertoire

Here are some free stroke parts that can be added to three pieces from Unit 1: Hot Cross Buns, Mary Had a Little Lamb, and Lightly Row. Practice playing these *IM* free stoke parts along with the melody, harmony, and bass parts.

Hot Cross Buns

Melody, harmony and bass part on p. 10

English Folk Song
arr. Johnny Peña

Chord Part

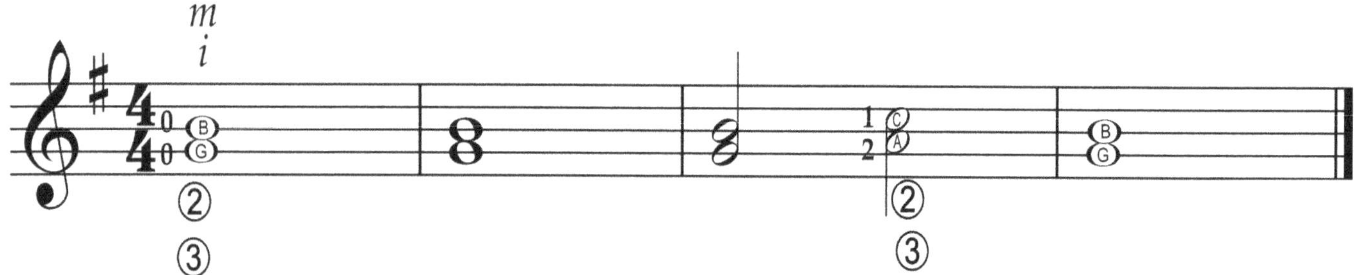

Mary Had a Little Lamb

Melody, harmony and bass part on p. 12

English Folk Song
arr. Johnny Peña

Chord Part

Lightly Row

Melody and harmony part on p. 14

German/English Folk Song
arr. Johnny Peña

Chord Part

Follow these steps for each part chord part:
1. Sing the solfege syllabes (or alphabet note names) and visualize the notes.
2. Sing and play with the right-hand only.
3. Sing and fret along with the left-hand only.
4. Play through the piece with both hands.

5th String A (La) and B (Ti)

These new notes will be incorporated into the upcoming bass line of "Viva Nova," which can be found on page 46.

A (La)
5th String

- The right-hand thumb (*p*) is planted on the 5th string.

B (Ti)
5th String
2nd Fret

- The left-hand 2nd finger presses down on the fret.

A Minor Scale

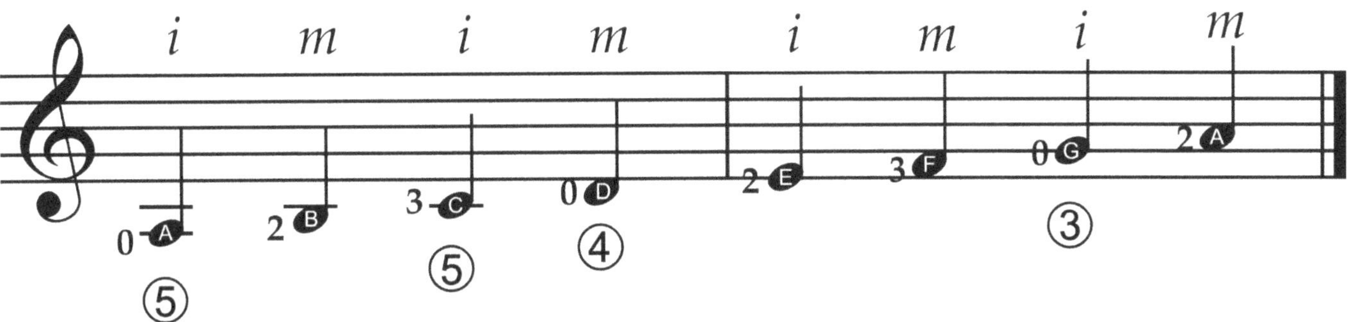

Notes used in this piece

La Ti Do Re Mi So La Ti Do Re

Viva Nova

♩=84

Johnny Peña

Melody

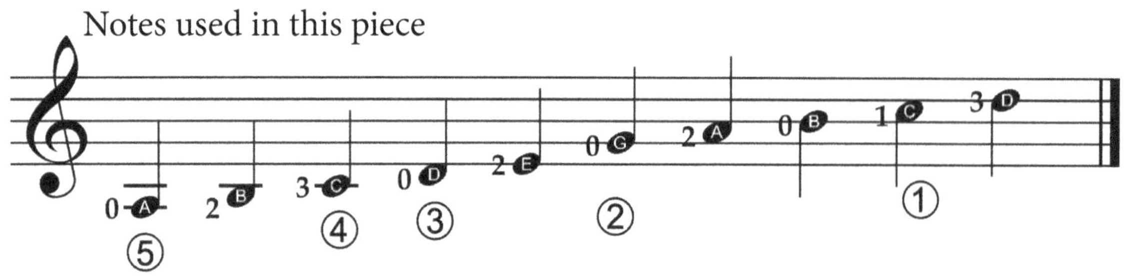

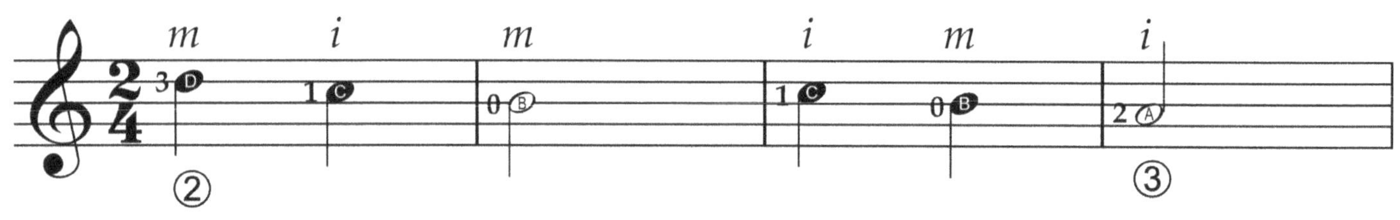

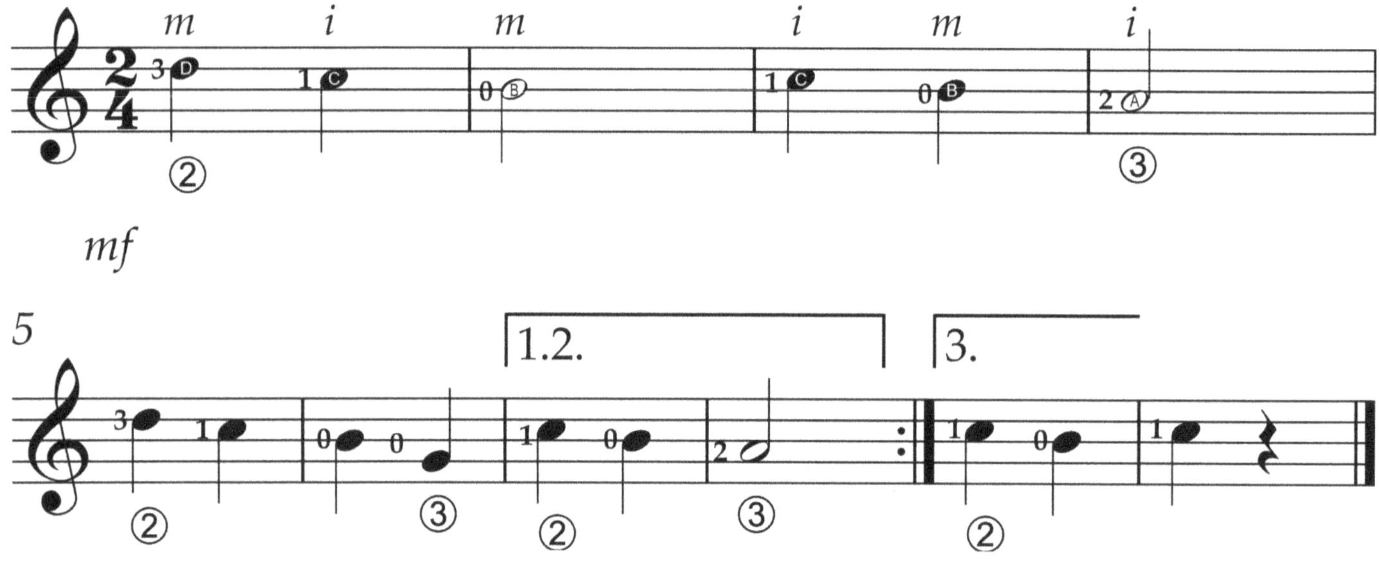

Bass

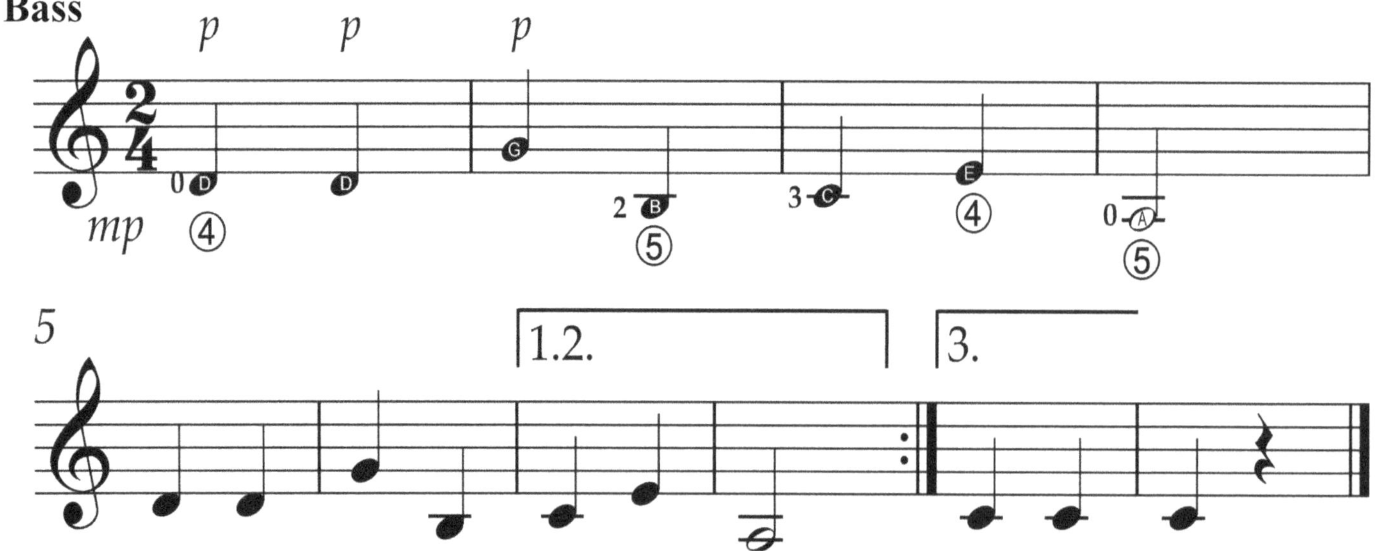

Chord Part

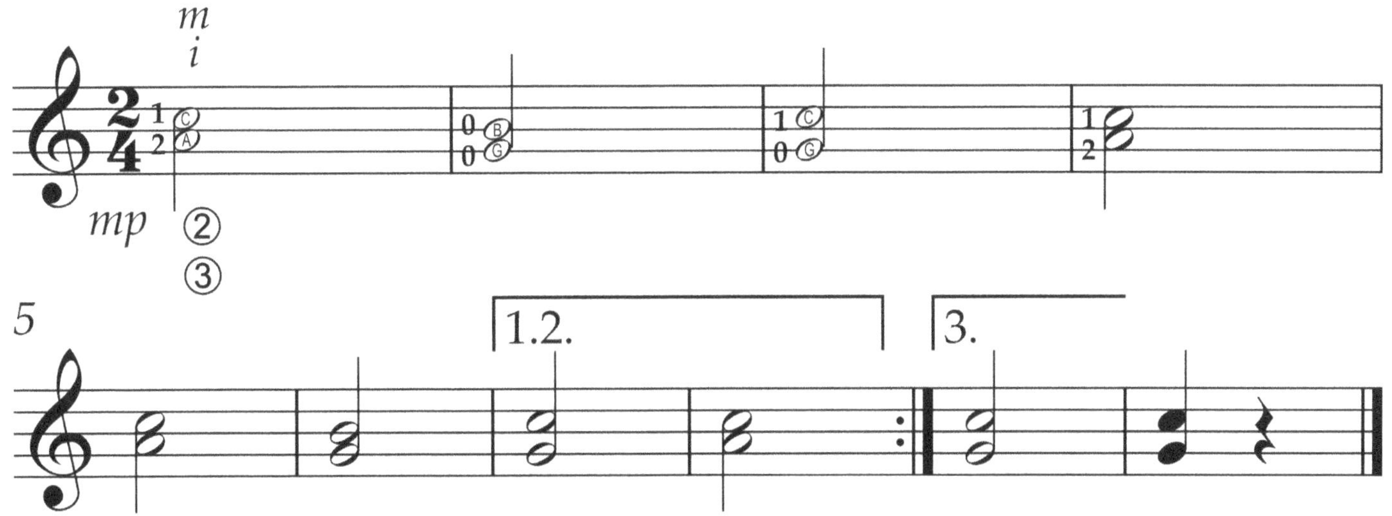

Teacher Accompaniment

Follow these steps for each part in Viva Nova:
1. Sing the solfege syllabes (or alphabet note names) and visualize the notes.
2. Sing and play with the right-hand only.
3. Sing and fret along with the left-hand only.
4. Play through the piece with both hands.

<u>1st String F# (Fi)</u>

This new note will be incorporated into the upcoming melody line of "French Folk Song," which can be found on page 49.

F# (Fi)
1st String
2nd Fret

- The left-hand 2nd finger presses down on the fret.

<u>G Major Scale</u>

Notes used in this piece

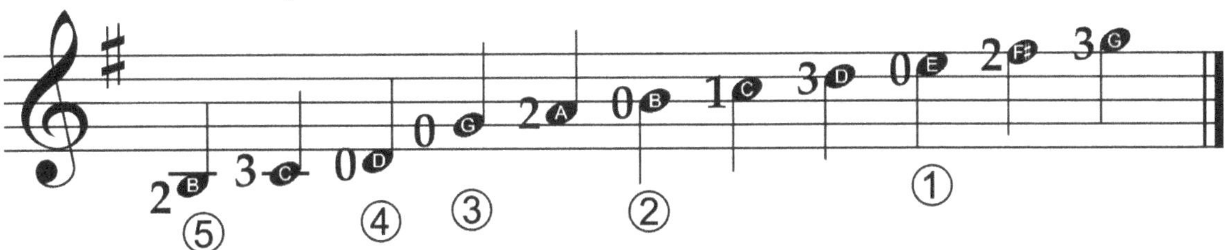

French Folk Song

Melody

French Folk Song
arr. Johnny Peña

French Folk Song

French Folk Song
arr. Johnny Peña

Bass

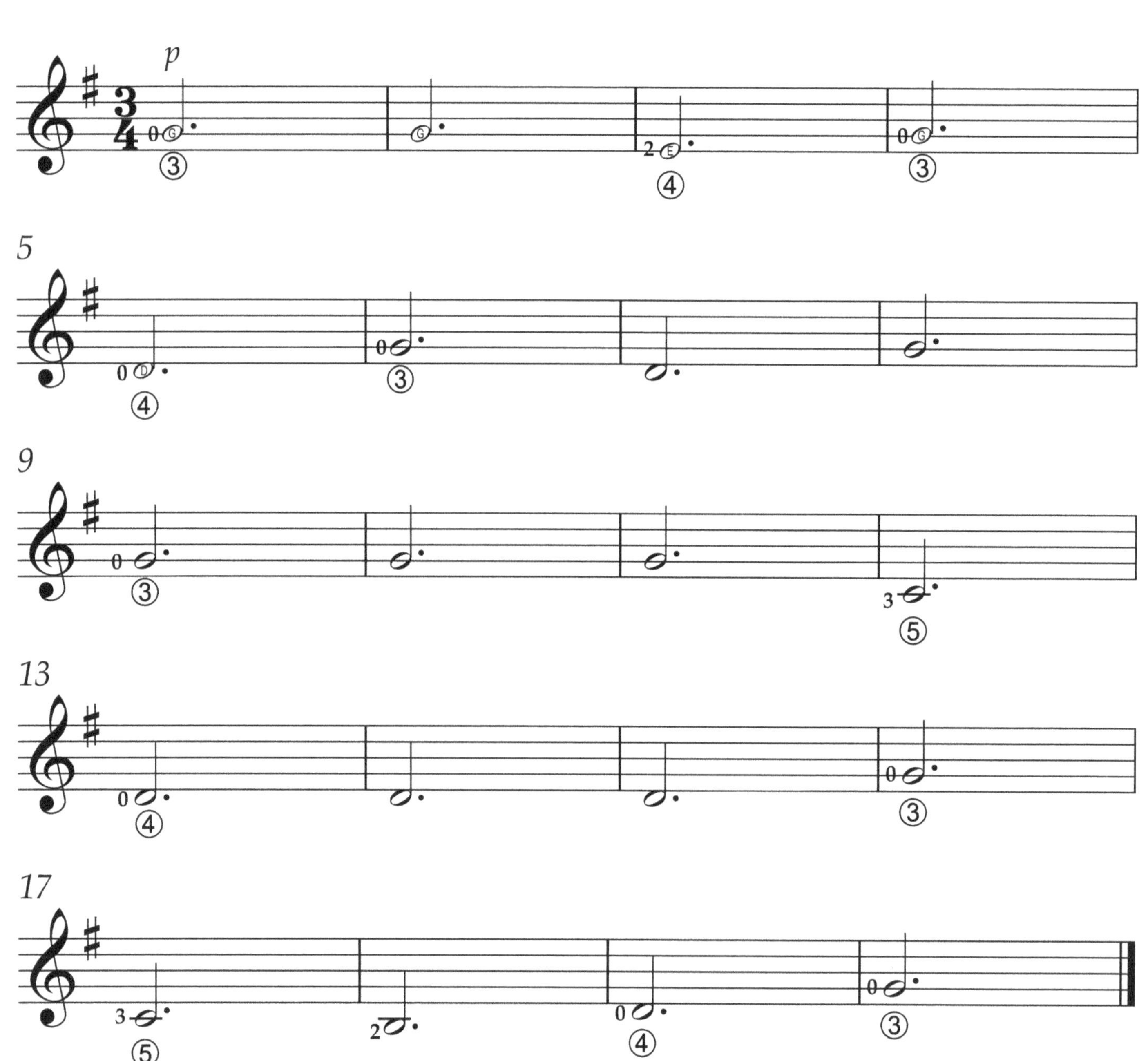

French Folk Song

Chord Part

51

French Folk Song

French Folk Song
arr. Johnny Peña

Teacher Accompaniment

This page is intentionally left blank.

3rd String and 5th String Bb (Te)

Bb (Te)
3rd String
3rd Fret

- The left-hand 3rd finger presses down on the fret.

Bb (Te)
5th String
1st Fret

- The left-hand 1st finger presses down on the fret.

Ex. 1

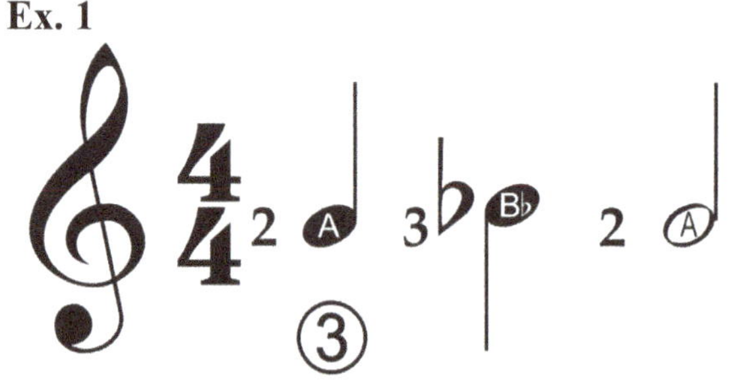

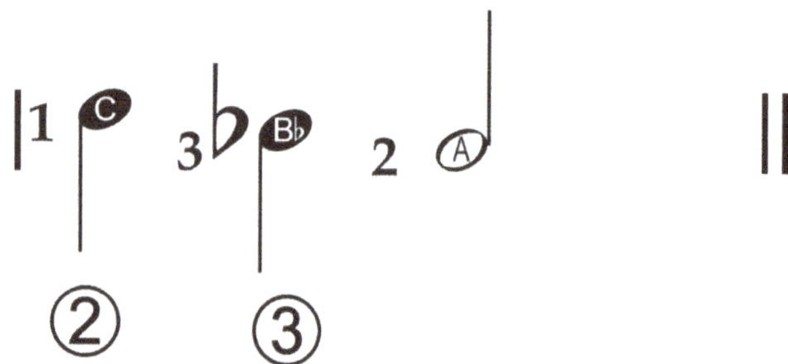

Ex. 2

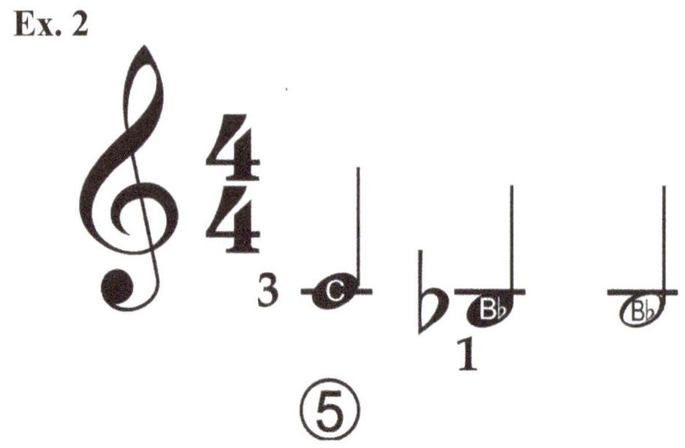

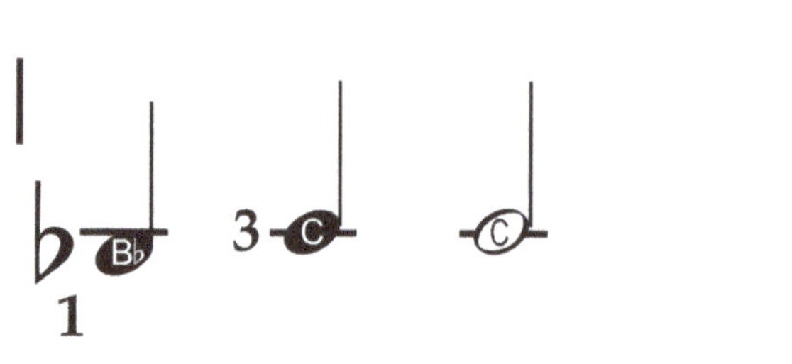

F Major Scale

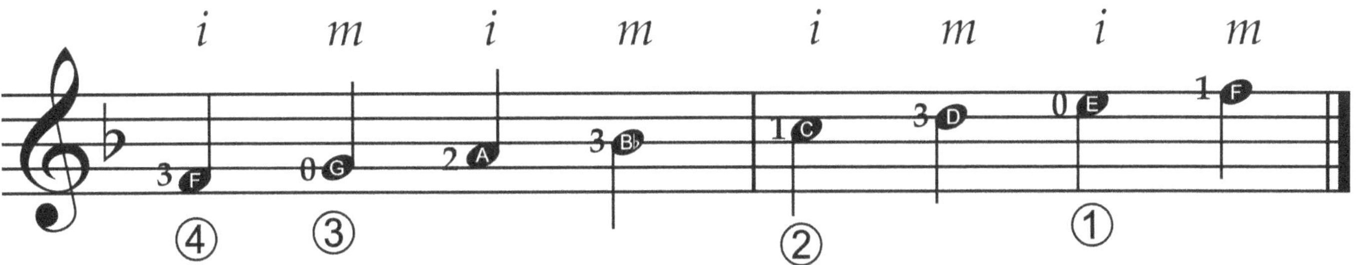

Notes used in this piece

Te Do Mi Fa So La Te Do Re

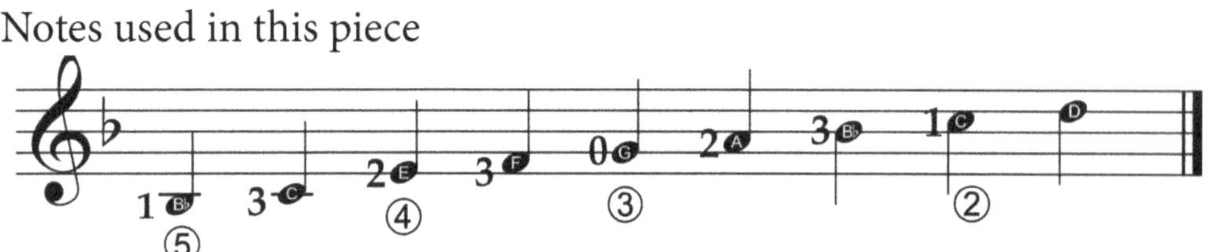

Brinca la Tablita

Mexican Folk Song
arr. Johnny Peña

Melody

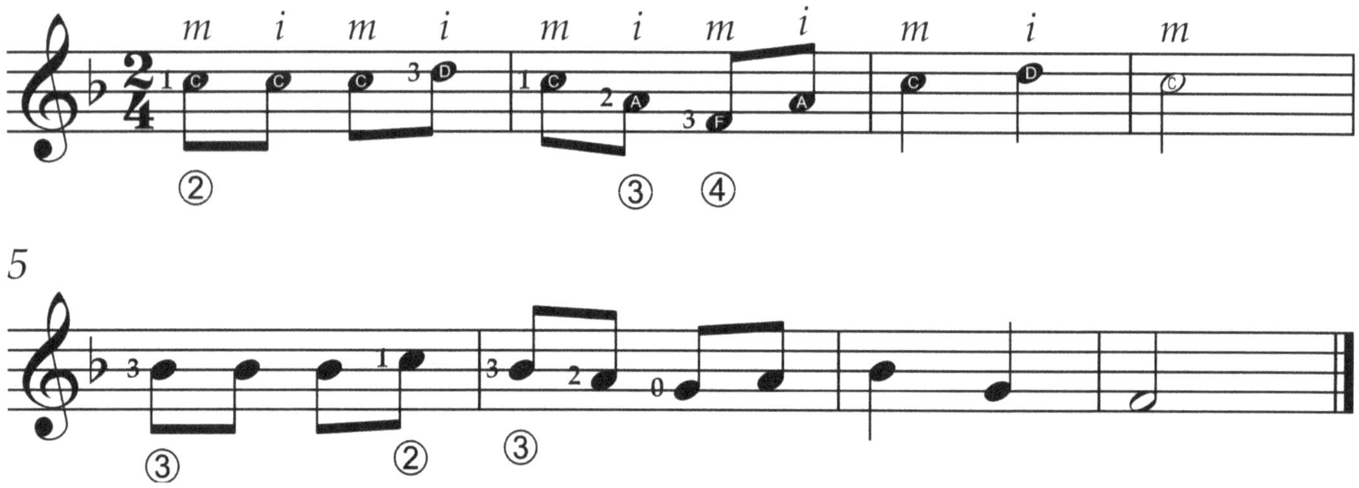

Harmony

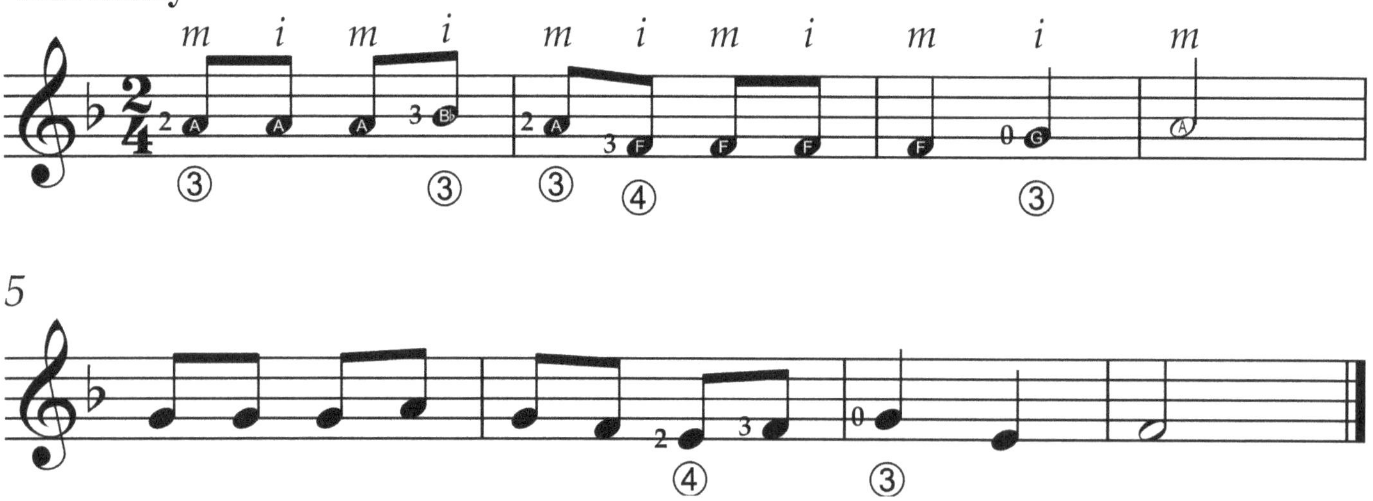

Follow these steps for each part in Brinca la Tablita:

1. Sing the solfege syllabes (or alphabet note names) and visualize the notes.
2. Sing and play with the right-hand only.
3. Sing and fret along with the left-hand only.
4. Play through the piece with both hands.

Bass

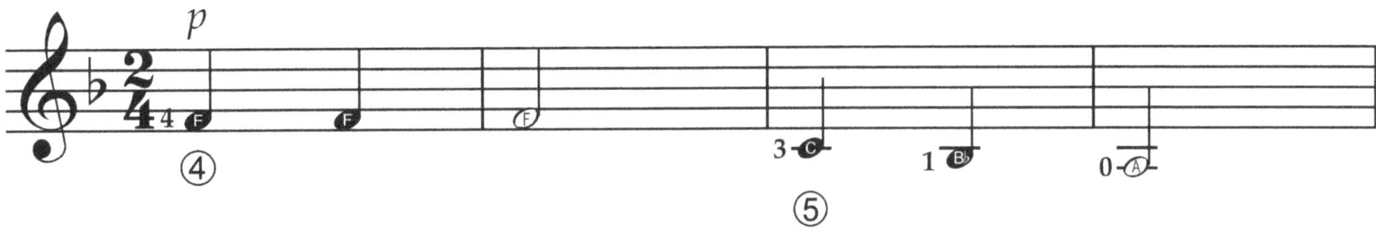

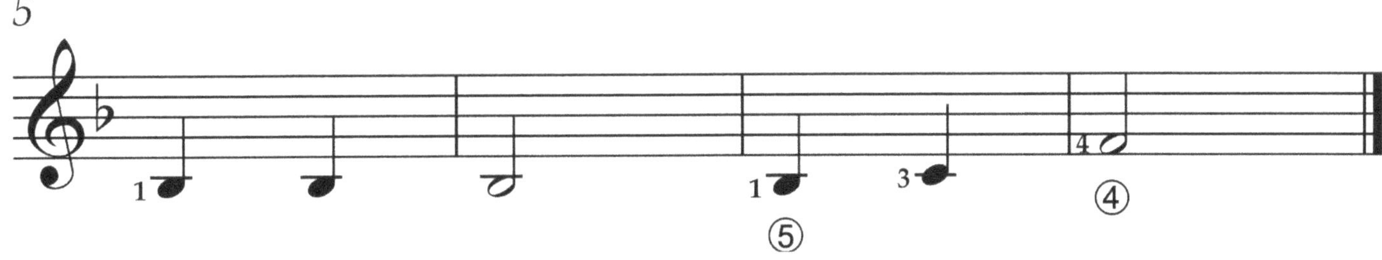

Chord Part

Brinca la Tablita- Teacher Accompaniment

D Minor Scale

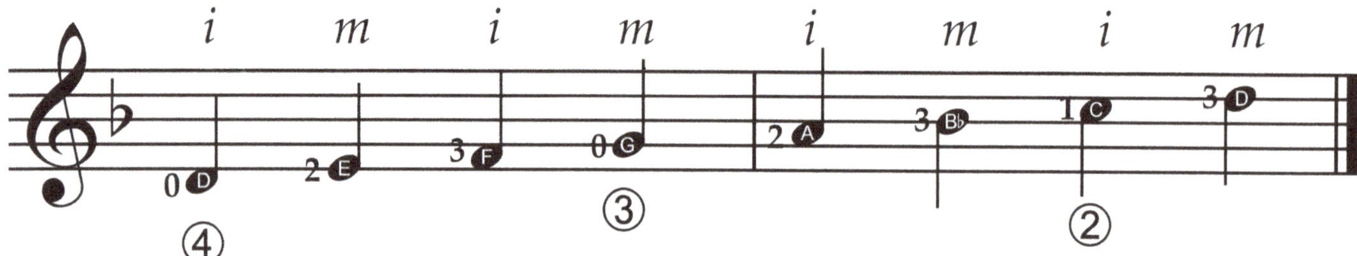

2nd String C

This new note will be incorporated into the upcoming piece titled "Ah Poor Bird," which can be found on page 59.

C# (Di)
2nd String
2nd Fret

- The left-hand 2nd finger presses down on the fret.

Notes used in this piece

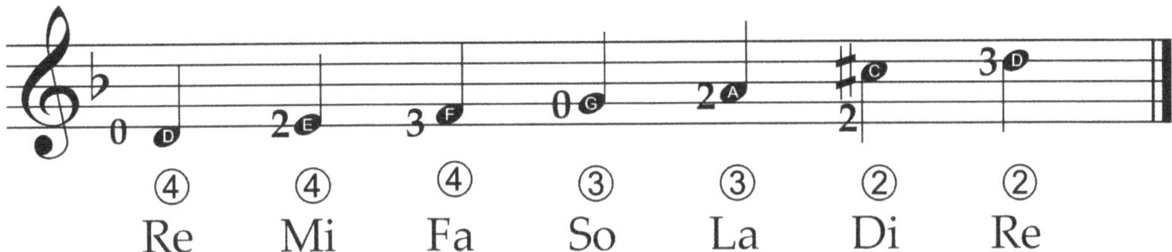

Ah Poor Bird
Round

English Folk Song
arr. Johnny Peña

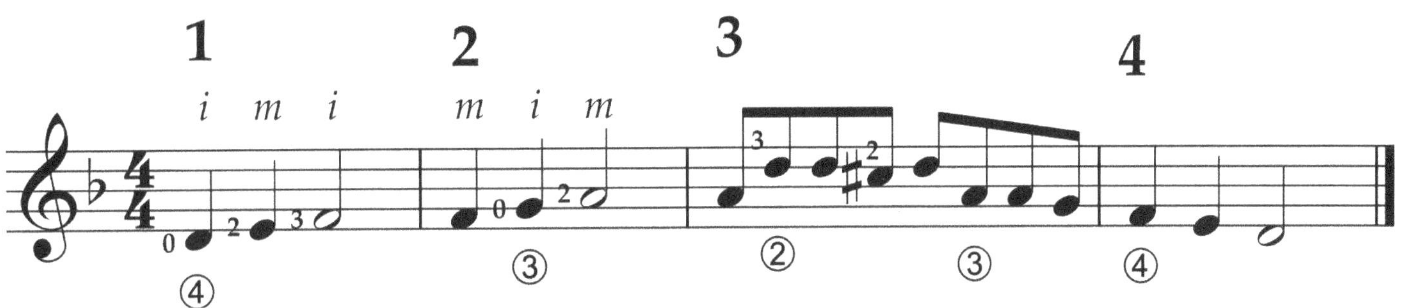

Follow these steps for each part in Ah Poor Bird:
1. Sing the solfege syllabes (or alphabet note names) and visualize the notes.
2. Sing and play with the right-hand only.
3. Sing and fret along with the left-hand only.
4. Play through the piece with both hands.

Shalom Chaverim
"Peace my friends till we meet again"

Israeli Folk Song
arr. Johnny Peña

Follow these steps for each part in Shalom Chaverim:
1. Sing the solfege syllabes (or alphabet note names) and visualize the notes.
2. Sing and play with the right-hand only.
3. Sing and fret along with the left-hand only.
4. Play through the piece with both hands.